# A Season for Everything

Jeen April Del Mundo Lay

BookLeaf Publishing

India | USA | UK

Presentation by *BookLeaf Publishing*

Web: www.bookleafpub.com

E-mail: info@bookleafpub.com

ISBN: 9789357691994

First edition 2022

# DEDICATION

To the love of my life - Daniel and Saoirse,

This wouldn't be possible if it weren't for the two of you.

To my Tatay and Inay, your wisdom made me pursue my love for writing.

# ACKNOWLEDGEMENT

In heaven, somebody must've been proud because I finally put my thoughts into writing - Atty. Casas, thank you for the inspiration.

# PREFACE

I have always been idealistic with just happiness coming my way. I did not expect that on being heartbroken and in pain, life can actually be beautiful and meaningful as well. Through my writings, I found purpose in what I believed were just miseries. Life has taught me that there is beauty in defeats, in grief, and mountains that I thought are insurmountable but actually, after looking closely, it taught me to be resilient, empowered, and brave. I hope readers can see through dilemmas and see the beauty in it.

# After Cinderella Left the Ball

She went back to the old her. She was in a sea of
emotions, a roller coaster ride of both sadness
and anxiety. The what ifs, the what could bes.
She was happy until the bell clang reminding her
that happiness has an ending too. Waking her up
that everything else was a part of an outlived
reality. There, she found herself trapped with
going back to the cinder, the slavery of thoughts
that she was stuck. That maybe if she only learnt
to speak up, things may be a little different.

Speak up. Voice out. Stop suppressing the
thoughts that enslave you from what other
people will think or say. It's time to brave the
gigantic fear that is trapped in your head. Live.
Live for you and not for anybody else.

# And then there was you

I thought I would reach the destination of never
finding you
There were doubts, fears, melancholy, and the
moroseness that in the dream of finding you,
I only found me...alone.

But God has His reason as to why I have to find
me before finding you.
He taught me to overflow with love so I can
show it to you.
Your abundance of patience and kindness left me
in awe.
I have never felt this loved and cared for the
entirety of my being.
You, my love, showed me how to be giving and
forgiving.
With the eternity that we're going to journey.
Know that I am with you, beside you,
completely.

# Ode to Saoirse

There were days when I ask myself why I was
given a daughter instead of sticking to being a
wife.
Because my entire world definitely changed
when you came into my life.
The ups and downs, twists and twirls make my
hair straight and curled.
My darling child, you are loaned to me by God
And trust me, I am clueless from the start.
On being your mum, my heart shattered and
shone at the same time.
For it is not a joke raising another human
especially someone I call mine.
My dearest Saoirse, years from now, you will
explore what will truly make you happy.
And whatever it is, your dad and I will always
make ourselves free to listen to your stories.
Our greatest joy will always be your arrival,
definitely worth the epidural!
Joking aside, I hope that you grow into a fine,
independent woman,
Surpassing any trials and defeats life may
overwhelm.
As you travel along the way, brave every storm.

Believe me when I say, God will help you and
the universe will conform.
Keep the faith, my love.
And grace will shower from above.

# Ode to Daniel

I didn't know angels exist until I met...

Driven by the universe conforming that
An angel like you will be given to lost,
wandering soul like mine
No one can compare the kind of love we have
found
In a moment of
Eureka flashing
Love is not fleeting; it intends to stay for the
lingest of time, an infinitum that either both of
us sees its sublimity.

(An acrostic poem for the love of my life)

# The Winds Have Changed

And that after all our exchange of thoughts, time
and effort,
I was right, you'll ghost me.
It wasn't even the 31st of October and yet, here I
am,
Trying to remember.
What I did wrong, why it was all gone.
You were gone without even calling you mine.
From the lovely May breeze, an autumnal you,
welcomed me by September.
I cannot even decipher as to why you walked
away.
Stay.
Please stay.
I didn't get the chance to mourn your walking
away.
I didn't get the chance to grieve this
brokenheartedness that I felt.
The winds have changed and all I can do was to
clothe me with hope that the next spring, I will
be okay.

# Springtime and Frappés

I remember sitting at the farthest left corner of the café.
I was bold. For someone with palpitations, I was bold enough to order me a coffee-based frappe.
I remember talking to you.
I was talking to you for about twenty minutes or so, telling you how I enjoy my free time doing nothing with you.
We talked without realising that it was already an hour and a half.
We were just having fun.
There were many times I neglect spending some good time with you,
Now that I have the chance, I kept it in my core.
You were having fun telling me how you loved frappés, too.
Your kicks and turns were tickles in my belly.
It was a beautiful springtime while my physique was seen as one, but in my heart, we are two.
Oops, your dad's waiting for us in the carpark.
Time for us to walk quite a distance
Because sooner than later, we'll walk hand in hand.
And we'll enjoy more cups of frappés and a whole lot of springtimes.

# The Perfect Fit

i think your eyes are like crystals
as i watch it glitter for the blankness of the
midnight
my head is resting on your arm
while we both held our bodies
as if it's a puzzle made to fit together
    you were never looking away
     so, i thought you'd stay
i think about how your scent is all over mine
from wearing your worn-out hoodie
the one with your favorite band printed on it
  and how warm you must have wanted me to
feel
before you leave me at dawn
on the coldness of the floor
sitting alone
and,
thinking about how the night
never ends in certain places
and how i desperately wish we were there
     at least for this to last

sometimes i think about
  how we hold so much on memories
like a found memorabilia

we store in our pocket spaces
  or a withered flower from a lover
we hide between the pages of our favorite book
    knowing we'll never get to keep
    something special like this again
so i close my eyes
and think
dream
visit.

# solitude


I should've told you that I love you
Because now I regret not saying it.

For in my thoughts and actions, you were always
the first that comes to mind.
How I wish I perfected a formulae where I was
bold enough to say what I wanted to say
While you're strong enough to stand up for me
So we would never be puzzled as to what we
feel about each other.

Under the maple tree, that red orange leaf fell on
my lap, I knew you were gone.
I know we are done.

# 12:00 a.m.

It's midnight and the rain started pouring.
With the cold breeze lingering in, I then played a
familiar song on my iPod.
It was a song you and I shared when we spent
the night by the beach - I was sober, you, drunk.
I laid in bed reminiscing...what could be us had
we chose to date each other.
There was a slight sigh I did, a sigh I know was
sure.
That night, when the moon was bright, the fire
was intense.
You grabbed my hand and put it on your
shoulder while yours slid on my waist.
The intro started, it was a sexy tune.
We started swaying, that first sway told me
something.
It was the regret of not being brave enough, bold
enough to tell me how you feel.
But on my defense, I should've done the same -
we should've fought hard enough until it's you
and I not me and him.
Tears started flowing from your eyes and mine.
We've forgotten the beat and lost the song.
Us is a memory now. We should've braved that
melody on that midnight.
I can still feel you're close to me and yet so far.

# Memoirs

It was all about you then
Time twisted and turned
It is now time to move on.

# Ghosts

It was a hot November day and my phone was in
complete silence
No more calls, no more texts received on my
end
That was when reality bit me with a hard truth,
yeah, we're over, we're done.
I thought resting included sleep alone
But my soul needed replenishing or another me
as a clone
While I was lying in bed, taming my feet
My phone started vibrating and saw a familiar
greet
It was someone in the past, taunting and
haunting
Like a predator who couldn't stop chasing
I, on the other end, was just asking what they
want
And all I received was litany full of rant
That they helped me chase after my goal,
And so I needed to pay them back from the
money I earned
From the beginning, I thought their kindness
was sincere
In the end, all they want was to dowse me in fear
But the lioness in me didn't get startled at all

For I know Madam Karma has its way to avenge
my fall
I paid the $550 in cash a day or two
Cut all connections and moved on with my life,
too
Wait, Madam K isn't finished with me yet
For she waited one year 'til my tolls are met
Their gruesome ending for me was divine
I no longer want to discuss the details
But trust me, you'll enjoy it with sips of
cocktails.

# First Date...maybe

The kind of whereabouts I want
Is the sight of you and I in it.
Moments like those make my heart flutter
I just wonder
Should I still reserve seats for two?
Because I know, at some point,
You'll consider a date with me, too.

# Peppermint Tea with the Divine

Most of the time, I often beg for things to
change
Like scenarios that could've been prevented
Had we tried our best at all.
There weren't many things that come to mind
that day
When you walked away.
I lost the best 7 years of you and I.
The scariest part of it all
Was to begin Day 1 without you in it,
As I try to reckon how can I fix it.
I was so clueless
So naive
That maybe if I was braver
We'll never reach to that part
that there's no more us
No more future
No more reminiscing the past.
I thought of leaving things behind me
By meeting the divine
Drinking coffee or tea beside them
Would definitely make me fine.
But one push of the divine
Helped me wake up from this nightmare

And now, the year has started with more
love and of taking care of me.
No more peppermint tea to remind me
How sad the previous year was
It's more of raspberry, lemon or strawberry
That lifted my spirit up
Now, in a nice way.

# A Story of a Damaged Body

If you would ask me how I was
I will tell you that one time
I opened my chest
to see what's wrong with me
There, I saw
My heart has grown a garden
From all the wounds you planted
How my liver reeks of alcohol
For I have been intoxicating myself every night
to forget
And, how my lungs would keep me from
Breathing in
Because I have been choking
With the last five words
Your mouth has uttered
Before walking away
"I thought I was ready."
I will tell you that one time
I was longing someone
To wrap a bandage around my ribcage
To fix me
Because I have been exploding inside too often
when you left
If you would ask me how I feel perhaps,
I will let you take over my body instead

Because hearing a story of how damaged it was
won't cause you any pain
To understand at all.

# Platonic Us

sometimes i see you
in crowded places,
like in that particular bookstore
where you saw me twice on christmas
now i'd always think of you when i go there
or sometimes remember you
from the faint smell of books,
or pens,
or maybe i just always picture you there
standing beside someone in that aisle of dusty
envelopes
and letters

you were always there
painted in sunsets
crazy orange and pink ones
in empty parking lots
where i used to drink iced coffees, now beers
while reading your texts
but now i don't get them anymore

you were always there
a name i never want to speak of when i am sober
but becomes an anecdote on my drunk stories

you were always there
and here i am always
standing five feet away from you
never wanting to leave too far from you
never wanting to forget
all the heartbreak stories i tell sunsets,
the collection of dried tears and cigarette filters
that reminds me of you

because maybe this is the closest i got
from being loved and i never want to
forget about that
you.

# Fairy Dusts

Just before leaving the apartment I rented for
several years,
I found a small, round tin
rusty, and hiding in the darkest area of my
closet.
Something looks familiar.
It was our beginning.
A memoir that has no end...at least for me.
I opened it and saw the tickets of the movies we
had watched,
    tickets of the concerts we had attended,
       receipts of the cafés we'd been to
        and some random post-its whenever one
of us didn't feel okay.
The thoughts of you still linger on these pieces
of paper,
like you're just around the corner of the street
waiting for me.
The dusts on the closet were like fairy dusts that
might answer my every whys.
You were my answered prayer.
But I won't be able to move on if I always cling
to what will no longer come back.
I look at it with the most passionate eyes
And then, it hit me.

The reality of you kicked in.
That an angel like you
will always look after me.

# The Leaves Have Fallen

The autumn colours are very vibrant
Leaving every road a mixture of red, orange and
brown
I quite like it.
It entails the end of summer
But after the cold breeze of December
Greeneries will again start to spring.
A new beginning.

# A Blank Page

Never in my wildest dreams
That a surprise would be given to me
For a sinner like me doesn't deserve it.
A tough feat and yet here I stand
God welcomes me with open arms
Cradled me to sleep
I was bathed with new hope and grace
I am a blank page.

# Finding Answers

The aroma of the coffee beans from the nearby
café
Reminded me that it's time to welcome you
The ground coffee that is bursting with flavour
A teaspoon of sugar, a little bit if milk
So I can still taste the bittersweet blend
Of the coffee you used to order for me
It was a part of my core memory.
I remember how you like your coffee.
Five minutes have passed and you popped by.
There was a little bit of palpitation
Or maybe it's the caffeine talking.
The anxiety of meeting you again
And maybe giving ourselves
Another chance to work things out.
But this time, instead of coffee.
I heard the barrista calling your name
For the looseleaf peppermint tea.
I know the answer already.

# Love in the Time of Covid

For years, I thought J was solely the problem.
With every failed relationship,
I know I was every bit of a pain.
There were times of self-pitying
But then I understood, that in every
Relationship one will have,
It's between you and the other person
Not you and you alone.
Cliché as it sounds,
It takes two to tango.
It takes two people to work things out.
After a year or two,
My previous partners would tell me
That I hinder their dreams.
That I was the problem.
That I was exhausting.
Then a man, out of my expectations, came.
Someone I didn't expect to meet...in person.
It was like Gabriel Garcia Marquez's Love in the
Time of Cholera
But ours was Covid.
There was an infinite number of differences,
Some, we refused to accept.
But I guess, fate wanted a different tune.

And we defied the thousand of miles and finally
met.
After the cheers and beers, a long exchange of
virtual calls and texts.
The man popped the question
And guess what, I said "yes".
Now, we're no longer two
But a family of three.
What more can you ask for?
Love costs no money, love is free.

# The Same Difference

Isn't it more interesting
When you and your partner have the same
differences?
Because that's what sets your uniqueness from
others.
Something that is rarely seen nowadays.
When you are set apart from the rest,
You stand out.
Isn't that more interesting than being the usual?
Even in the most crowded areas
Of the noisiest people around,
There will always be YOU
Who'll stand forth and brave the eyes
That judge every other person in that space.